M000238055

THE HISTORICAL CASITAS

OF

LA QUINTA COVE

SPANISH COLONIAL REVIVAL 1935 – 1941

Maggie Gordon

WRITTEN AND COMPILED BY MAGGIE GORDON

PHOTOGRAPHY BY MAGGIE GORDON

Copyright © 2007 by Maggie Gordon

All rights reserved. No part of this book shall be reproduced or transmitted in any form or by any means, electronic, mechanical, magnetic, photographic including photocopying, recording or by any information storage and retrieval system, without prior written permission of the publisher. No patent liability is assumed with respect to the use of the information contained herein. Although every precaution has been taken in the preparation of this book, the publisher and author assume no responsibility for errors or omissions. Neither is any liability assumed for damages resulting from the use of the information contained herein.

ISBN 0-7414-3937-9

Published by:

1094 *New Dehaven Street, Suite 100*
West Conshohocken, PA 19428-2713
Info@buybooksontheweb.com
www.buybooksontheweb.com
Toll-free (877) BUY BOOK
Local Phone (610) 941-9999
Fax (610) 941-9959

Printed in the United States of America
Printed on Recycled Paper
Published August 2007

FOREWORD

The long-awaited research on the Cove casitas is finished.

Along with the historic homes in Palm Springs, the La Quinta Cove casitas were the Coachella Valley's first private getaways.

The casitas are sheltered under the mantle of the beautiful surrounding mountains.

Living in La Quinta, many experience an aura of peace and the feeling of serenity. The closeness to nature, with the sounds of the quail and the mourning dove, makes the Cove a special place.

Yes, happy is the owner of a treasured casita.

Louise Neeley
Historian
La Quinta Historic Museum manager

DEDICATION

This book is dedicated to three special people in appreciation of their combined extraordinary talents and respect for the restoration of our 1937 casita.

Judith Schultz is my childhood friend and a gifted designer from Lodi, California. Judi rolled up her sleeves and taught us how to approach our project with a plan. Then she launched us into the remodeling project.

Mark Turvell is a competent and ethical local contractor with an appreciation of Mexican architecture and an amiable sense of humor. Mark restored our old casita into a magical place.

Alvaro Melendrez is an outstanding landscaper who transformed our bare yard into an inviting sanctuary for birds, butterflies and us.

Judi, Mark and Al,
This book is dedicated to YOU!

TABLE OF CONTENTS

CHAPTER ONE

THE CASITAS

Deep in the Colorado Desert of Southern California lies the City of La Quinta. Tucked away in a cove surrounded by the Santa Rosa Mountains are 63 small houses with red tile roofs, mostly hidden behind adobe-like walls.

The exceptional thing is that these little houses were all built between 1935 and 1941. They are all related by their modest size, white adobe-like exterior, low, red-tiled roofs, paned windows, and wooden lintels. To the outside world, all that is seen is the tops of their red roofs.

They are mysterious and charming to outsiders. Who built these homes? Who lived in them? Why are they sprinkled around the cove without rhyme or reason? There is a story, and there is a colorful past.

Early La Quinta Cove before World War II (photo courtesy of L.Q. Historical Museum).

Spanish Colonial Revival – 1937. Casitas were tucked away behind adobe-like walls, nestled in the cove of the Santa Rosa Mountains. This is one of 63 red-tiled roof casitas sprinkled around the La Quinta Cove

CHAPTER TWO

PRE-LA QUINTA: 1900 – 1932

Before 1902, the La Quinta Cove was part of the hunting grounds for the Cahuilla Indians. This was proven by the countless arrowheads found in and around this area by the settlers. The cove was as nature had preserved it for millions of years. Then, in 1902, John Marshall from Los Angeles cleared 160 acres for farmland at the west end of what is now Washington Avenue.

In 1927, Walter Morgan built the La Quinta Hotel at the north of the cove. He also planted Deglet Noor dates. Around the Santa Rosa mountain range at highway 111 and Washington Avenue, Mr. Clark, who owned the Point Happy Ranch, had purchased 11 Arabian horses. He had plans to crossbreed them with Scotch Hunter horses to produce exceptional polo ponies.

The land was vast and the population was sparse. The La Quinta Cove was known as Marshall's Cove. Washington Avenue was then known as Marshall Road.

The La Quinta Hotel was named at a party when a local rancher, Raymond Pedersen, told Morgan and friends of a hacienda in Mexico called La Quinta. Not only was the Hotel named La Quinta; in 1982, the city was named La Quinta, and the cove area is now called the La Quinta Cove.

Transportation to this desert area was by Southern Pacific Railroad into Indio. From there, a car from the Hotel would arrive to pick up guests. Later, small private aircraft could fly into the small airstrip located adjacent to the Hotel. Automobiles could drive on the partially maintained roads to this isolated place.

The Hollywood studios would drive the stars and starlets out to the La Quinta Hotel for rest and relaxation. Eisenhower Street was then known as Serra. In 1932, with the arrival of La Quinta's first developer, the cove was in for a change.

Wildflowers in the beautiful, natural, undeveloped La Quinta cove (photo courtesy of L.Q. Historical Museum).

CHAPTER THREE

E. S. "HARRY" KIENER: The Developer

E.S. "Harry" Kiener of the Big Bear Land and Water Company arrived in the La Quinta area in 1932. Kiener purchased several thousand acres around the La Quinta Hotel, including the cove area. His plan was to develop the cove area to complement his summer hunting and fishing resort in the mountains of Big Bear. Guests or owners of each area would have reciprocal privileges to enjoy the winter months in the warm desert of La Quinta and enjoy the summer months in the cool San Bernardino Mountains at the Peter Pan Woodland Club. The original use was for members only as described below. This excerpt from his marketing material explains the plan:

> "All of these facilities are to be enjoyed under the Pioneer Memberships, which can be acquired only by active members of PETER PAN WOODLAND CLUB. Here are the ultimate in reciprocal club privileges the year round...Peter Pan throughout the summer...THE DESERT CLUB throughout the winter...each club complete and distinctive within itself...each the perfect compliment of the other."

Kiener created the Palm Springs – La Quinta Development Company. The cove subdivision was formally called the Santa Carmelita de Vale subdivision. The streets were laid out in a grid pattern bounded by Calle Tampico on the north, Avenida Bermudas on the east, Calle Tecate on the south, and Avenida Montezuma and Bear Creek on the west.

The first La Quinta subdivision as approved by Riverside County 1933-37 (Courtesy of L.Q. Historical Museum).

La Quinta cove was subdivided in 1933-1937 to become the first subdivision in what was later to be the City of La Quinta. Dr. Ralph Pawley, a local physician, wrote about flash floods in the cove. Julie Hirsch in "Remembering the Desert Club" tells about the silt covering an entire orchard, found only when the Desert Club swimming pool was being excavated by hand. Kiener had huge challenges to overcome the flooding problems. Wendy Lemmons, a resident from the 1950's, tells of large berms down the center of the cove streets to help reduce drainage from the flash floods.

Kiener's plan was to build small, charming weekend casitas to architecturally match the very successful and popular La Quinta Hotel. The subdivision was deliberately spread out to ensure low density development of the little Spanish houses made of stucco, roof tiles, and decorative ceramic tiles, imitating the materials used in Mexico. A club would be constructed as an incentive offering for those who would purchase home sites and homes in the La Quinta Cove development. In his advertisement, Kiener made the following claims:

> "The ultimate in Clubdom...THE DESERT CLUB...to be erected at La Quinta, California...providing a wealth of pastimes and desert sports...superbly appointed in a housing ultra-modern...privately secluded in a mountain sheltered cove...an empire of natural beauty...yet but a few minutes from business centers...dedicated to luxurious recreation and rest...devoted to the exclusive use of its members."

On Montezuma, across from the current park, a two-story office building was erected. This housed the La Quinta Milling and Lumber Company on the ground floor and the contractor's family on the second floor. The lumberyard was in the back of the structure. The administration building for sales and marketing was built next door. Today, the La Quinta Historical Society and Museum is located in that building.

The Palm Springs –La Quinta Development Company administration building, 1936. The La Quinta Milling and Lumber Company is in the background. This is the office where sales and rentals took place for the casitas (photo courtesy of L.Q. Historical Museum).

This is a reprint of an advertisement by the Palm Springs – La Quinta Development Company, which offers opportunities in ownership and membership in the Desert Club at La Quinta (Courtesy of L.Q. Historical Museum).

The construction of the casitas began in 1935. In addition to the four homes that were completed that year, concrete street markers were designed and installed. The three and one half foot tall markers were placed diagonally on the street corners. The street names were attached to the top on enameled name plates, which rested on steel markers set in concrete. Later, the names were written down the sides of the concrete posts, as you see them today.

Concrete street marker, 1935. This is the original design (photo courtesy of Victor Teran).

Modern-day concrete marker with the street name down the side, concrete base 1935.

In 1935, the 50x100 (or sometimes 50x150) lots sold for $195. Kiener sold the weekend homes for $2,500. They were completely furnished, right down to the linens.

Casita, 1939 (Photo Courtesy of L.Q. Historical Museum).

Julie Scott Hirsch's first home in Avenida Vallejo, 1937 (Photo courtesy Julie Scott Hirsch).

1936 casita. This picture was taken in the 1950s (photo courtesy Victor Teran).

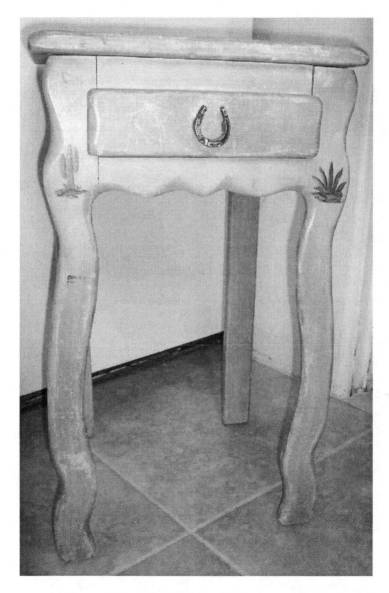

1935-1940 original furnishings: nightstand

1935-1940 original furnishings: chair and ottoman made of hardwood with iron decorative trim

1935-1940 original furnishings: coffee table made out of hardwood with iron decorative trim.

1935-1940 original painting from a fully furnished casita.

Early La Quinta Cove, before World War II (Photo courtesy of L.Q. Historical Museum).

CHAPTER FOUR

ARCHITECTURAL STYLE: Spanish Colonial Revival

The Cove casitas were modeled after the charming, romantic La Quinta Hotel. The Spanish Colonial Revival style has never lost its charm. The style is romantic, yet humble, using natural materials of stucco, clay tiles, and iron. These little homes have a balance between austerity and ornamentation. They mimic adobe construction. There is an intimate relationship to the environment because of their handcrafted nature. Patios, archways, and some exposed beams or slightly vaulted ceilings help give a sense of informality and warmth.

Original "peek door" in the front door.

Original latch.

Original 3-panel bedroom door.

Original 3-panel bathroom door.

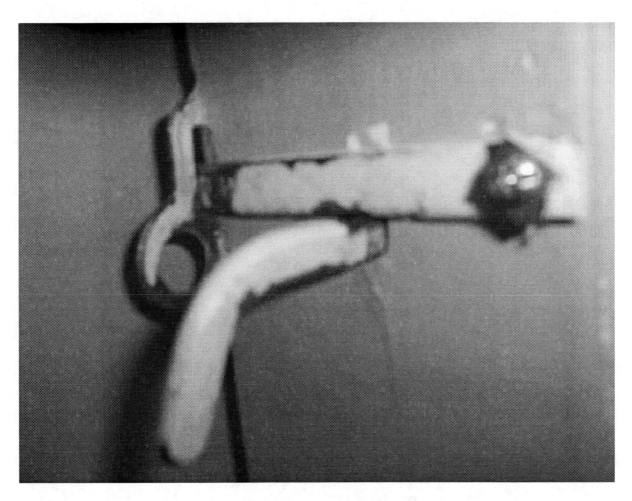

Original bathroom door latch.

Original fireplace.

The little houses were well built, using natural materials that develop character rather than decay as they age. The red roof tiles develop characteristic patinas as they age. The original tiles were made locally by the Joe Valenzuela Roof Company, which was located next to the La Quinta Hotel. Valenzuela also made the roof tiles for the Hotel using local clay.

Original roof tiles made by Joe Valenzuela Roof Company.

Old red tiles and decorative supports from 1937.

Original open decorative supports under roof.

Original lintel and three old vigas under slanting shed roof.

Original roof tiles, still in good condition.

Old rock wall in backyard. Looks like stones collected from the base of the Santa Rosas.

There are two basic floor plans, the "I" shape and the "L" shape. Both floor plans have the red-tiled roofs, wooden lintels over the garage or carport openings, stucco walls, and multi-paned casement windows. The chimneys are short and slightly tapered with a top. Most of the homes are single-story houses with low, pitched roofs, cross gable roofs, or half hip or shed. Some homes have a central patio in the front and wing wall. The garage and entry doors have the Z, or strap wood, design.

All the casitas are modest in scale, with one, two, or three bedrooms. Most casitas were built with a carport or a garage. Over the past 70 years, these "weekend" homes have been modernized to accommodate family needs and full-time living. Some owners have merged the original 50x100 foot lot with one or two vacant lots next door. Most owners have landscaped and added an adobe-like wall, wooden fence, or hedge screen around their properties.

The casitas were built in an irregular order on random lots sprinkled throughout the Cove with no rhyme or reason. Often, the buyers could select their desired lot location.

Original "Z" style front door.

Original "Z" front door, center patio, double hung windows.

CHAPTER FIVE

MARKETING – 1933-1947 (and later)

In 1935, the marketing plan was designed to target the owners and users of the Peter Pan Club in Bear Valley, enticing them with the same club amenities. Kiener felt a recreation club, restaurant and swimming complex would be necessary to attract buyers and renters to this remote but beautiful winter oasis. Here is an excerpt from "Remembering the Desert Club:"

> "The recreational facilities of the DESERT CLUB are scheduled to include a swimming pool, tennis and badminton courts, archery range, riding stables and ring, modern equipment for sun bathing, card lounge, dining room, coffee shop, billiard and card rooms, landscaped patios and terraces.
>
> When you own a home at lovely La Quinta, your cup of happiness is full and overflowing. For here a bit of desert wasteland has been transformed into a garden of Eden. Your life is leisurely, lazy, luxurious. In dungarees, dude-ranch togs or dress-up dinner clothes, you live like a king. If you are sports minded there are swimming, tennis, badminton, croquet, ping-pong and archery on the close-by-grounds...with horseback riding, cycling at hand in Vale La Quinta. ...It's next door to heaven; our fondest dream come true.
>
> La Quinta and the Desert Club where winter never comes."

The building of the homes began in 1934. The Desert Club opened on Thanksgiving Day, 1937. Guests of the La Quinta Hotel were among the first to be offered the opportunity to own a piece of La Quinta. Alan Ladd, Shirley Booth, Bob Cummings, Tom Mix, a Broadway producer, doctors and lawyers from Southern California, and many more stars and starlets became owners or regular guests.

The Desert Club with the Santa Rosa Mountains as the perfect backdrop (Photo Courtesy of the L.Q. Historical Museum).

During World War II, homes could not be built, but developers were allowed to sell lots. In 1943, a brochure, "Presenting La Quinta," was printed as a marketing tool. Now, the cove is being referred to as "Vale La Quinta." Mr. Kiener became ill in 1936. His four salesmen, Louis Berkowitz, Walter Hast, Frank Stone and Edward Glick, had invested in the project, and they took ownership.

Stone and Glick called their business the "Palm Springs Land and Irrigation Company." They began a very aggressive marketing campaign, changing with the times, opening up the lot and home sales not only to the Peter Pan owners but to all interested non-member parties as well.

The war years shut down The La Quinta Hotel. The La Quinta area was like a ghost town according to one resident, Robert Stoliker.

Here is a reprint from the 1943 brochure, "Presenting La Quinta:"

"Every year the mecca of thousands [come to the desert] seeking the sunshine, beauty and dry, health-giving climate of the desert. La Quinta has earned an international reputation as America's foremost desert resort community....Deep in the midst of California's world-famous desert lies a beautiful cove, made by the sturdy hands of Mother Nature...Vale La Quinta... a paradise sheltered by huge, towering mountain ranges on three sides. All of La Quinta is zoned – wisely and with full appreciation of future development, its needs and requirements....It features low, brilliantly trimmed, white stucco structures that gleam with picturesque splendor in the clear, desert sun against a background of stately mountain ranges, delicately tinted with the mauves and purples of afternoon shadows.

Utilities are here...electricity and telephone service...the water supply is most plentiful and is of unusual clearness, purity, and entirely free from contamination.

LOCATION...Geographically, it is the logical center of a new reclamation area and a rapidly growing agricultural empire.

TRANSPORTATION...The main line of the Southern Pacific Railroad passes through Indio, eight miles distant. From here a paved highway leads to La Quinta. Paved motor roads also connect the community with Los Angeles and San Diego. And with established airport facilities, the village is within rapid flying time of Southern California cities.

CLIMATE...With the exception of the four months from June to September when the weather is rather warm, La Quinta boasts ideal atmospheric conditions...

OILS AND MINERALS...They may be there, but the sponsor company makes no reservations of such rights in its deeds.

HEALTH...World renowned for its sunshine and the freshness of its dry desert air, La Quinta has long been recognized for its restorative powers. Thus, numerous physicians have endorsed the therapeutic value of its climate.

IMPROVEMENTS...Streets, water, electricity are installed at the expense of the sponsor company. Water is made available for domestic use and streets are surfaced in conformance with the requirements of Riverside Planning Commission. The water system which is owned by the Santa Carmelita Mutual Water Company, consists at present of three wells, a reservoir having a capacity of 170,000 gallons and approximately 22 miles of pipe line. Electrically operated pumps force the water through the mains, which are from two to ten inches in diameter. The wells, constructed with 12-inch double casing, are capable of producing more than sufficient water for the community. At its own expense the sponsor company planted about 1500 trees throughout the civic center and along the streets. The trees have since been taken over by the water company and are cared for by it, and an additional planting program is now being planned. Plans are also under way for the oil surfacing by the Mutual Water Company of additional streets throughout the community. Modern, sanitary septic tanks solve the sewage problem; cesspools are not permitted. Enameled name plates resting on steel markers set in concrete, make for easy street identification.

RESTRICTIONS...Deeds issued by the Palm Springs Land and Irrigation Co. contain protective clauses insuring the erection of pleasant and harmonious buildings. Ownership, use and occupancy are restricted to the Caucasian race."

Today, in 2007, it is absurd that anyone could have ever thought that he or she could isolate an entire Californian community with one race. In the 1930's, though, that was the mentality. Our modern attitudes and ways have improved and enriched our society and our communities.

"ANTICIPATED PROFITS...The company anticipates a steady growth and an increase in values of the property throughout the area. It does not expect or promise an immediate "overnight" boom. But it does feel, however, that in presenting La Quinta properties at extremely low prices, it is making possible a substantial margin of future profit for present investors.

LA QUINTA AS A COMMUNITY has been planned and built under the requirements of the Riverside County Planning Commission. The California Real Estate Commissioner has issued an Inspection Report, a copy of which we require to be shown to every prospective purchaser."

The movie stars, the wealthy, and the famous visitors were used in the marketing material for Vale La Quinta. These quotations are reprinted from the 1943 brochure, "Presenting La Quinta:"

"Excerpt from an article written by Cornelius Vanderbilt, Jr., appearing in the *Liberty Magazine* of February 27, 1937: "Twenty miles away" [from Palm Springs] "La Quinta, one of the most beautiful desert resorts in the world, shows a 50 per cent increase in business over the same period in 1936."

Excerpts from an article, "Why Movie Stars Hide Out in the Desert," written by 'Liza' and appearing in the *Screenland* Magazine for May, 1939: "If a doctor told me I had only ten months to live...I would choose to spend my ten months at the desert resort of La Quinta, stretched out in a sun suit beneath a date palm, drinking in the breath-taking beauty of the Santa Rosa Mountains.

La Quinta is neither homespun nor chummy – and here you find the movie stars who honest-to-goodness meant it when they said they wanted to 'get away from it all'.

As far as Hollywood is concerned, it was Garbo who 'discovered' this fascinating place which has all the fascinating mystery and beauty of the desert...but it was probably the late Marie Dressler who made it a popular rendezvous of the Hollywood folks who wanted a place in which they might vacation in peace.

Others who love the peace and beauty of La Quinta and who like to relax without benefit of camera, are Ronnie Colman and Benita Hume, Merle Oberon, Miriam Hopkins, Brian Aherne, Joel McCrea and Frances Dee, the Spencer Tracys, Errol Flynn and Lili Damita, Joan Blondell and Dick Powell, Dolores Del Rio and Cedric Gibbons, Gladys Swarthout and Frank Chapman, Una Merkel and Ronnie Burla, Leslie Howard, and George Brent...And it is here Eddie Cantor often whips into shape his radio program, and Irving Berlin the songs for his next picture.

Excerpts from an article entitled "California (Not Hollywood)," written by "Alajalov," and appearing in the January 1, 1937, issue of *Vogue*: "And there's the desert – sun-blanched, hairy, austere in form with constant chameleon-like changes of colour. La Quinta is the most charming place in it -Gloria Swanson always goes there, and the charming Mrs. Nathaniel B. Potter from New York spends a few months of every winter there...It's a place for complete rest and relaxation, a place to catch up on your reading. (The air is supposed to do wonders with you.)

If La Quinta is comme-il-faut, near-by Palm Springs is definitely in danger of soon becoming comme-il-ne-faut-pas.

By 1947 The Desert Club was being promoted nationally in *Fortune* Magazine...Land of Enchantment for your dream home. Within a whisper of Palm Springs...3 hours from Los Angeles...lies secluded La Quinta, California's smartest year-round desert playground. Here, in a sun-kissed setting of Nature's own incredible Technicolor contrasts, is the ultra-smart Desert Club and the carefully zoned, long established home site development with its alluring opportunities for investment or ideal living. For a club vacation in dungarees or dress clothes, or for building that cherished home of your dreams, golden hours really 'out of this world' are yours...at lovely, lazy, luxurious La Quinta."

A horseback ride through the La Quinta Cove (Photo courtesy of the LQ Historical Museum).

1937 "L" design. Spanish Colonial Revival with Pueblo Revival influences. Multi-level shed roof of red clay tiles and large wooden lintel.

1937 "L" shape. The top of the "L" is adorned by three vigas placed directly underneath the slanting roof line.

1937. This roof looks like the original with a low-pitched, front gabled roof line. Exposed rafters end at the eaves. Vertical wood planking fills in the gables.

1937 "L" shaped Spanish Colonial Revival with pueblo revival details. A wooden lintel over original wooden double doors, "Z" timbers.

1937 casita on four lots. You can barely see the low, red-tiled roof line.

1936 casita hidden by a wonderful old front gate covered with a vibrant crimson blooming Bougainvillea. Old tiles in steps and old gate light.

This old iron decorative gate is hiding a 1936 casita on a double lot.

This 1937 casita hidden by vegetation and an adobe-like wall all around.

1936 casita hidden from the street by vegetation and a low, adobe-like wall.

1937 casita hidden by an adobe-like wall trimmed with red brick straddling an old wooden gate.

1936 "L" shape casita. Complex shed style red tile roof. Chimney has a short stack.

1937 large casita on two lots. Part of the red-tiled roof is original.

1936 casita, "I" shape. Most of the casitas originally had a center front patio.

Low red-tiled roof casita hidden from the street. Short chimney stack with a top.

Modernized casita still hidden from the street.

1936 "H" shape casita, modernized but maintains wings, shed roof, four vigas, and the large wooden lintel.

1937 casita has a shed roof, low-pitched red-tiled roof, and original wooden garage doors with upper vents still in place.

1939 casita.

1936 casita.

1938 casita.

1937 casita with lintel over window.

Low, red-tiled roof.

1936 "I" shape casita with shed roof.

1939 casita enjoyed by four generations of the same family.

The same 1939 casita that was on the previous page, this photo was taken in the 1950s (photo courtesy of Wendy Lemmons).

1940 casita with mature trees and cactus plantings, multi-paned windows, and stucco with a red-tiled roof.

1948 casita totally hidden by shrubs except for the low, red-tiled roof. This casita was built after WWII.

CHAPTER SIX

WORLD WAR II: CHANGE

In 1936, when the age-old desert land on the east side of Southern California was as primitive and pristine as it had been for a million years, the management of Palm Springs – La Quinta Development Company envisioned a colony of Spanish Colonial style casitas and club life that would rank as one of the finest in California.

A series of unexpected major events took place. Mr. Kiener, the promoter and developer, who had been ill for several years, suddenly died of a heart attack. The war broke out, and all building stopped. Materials became scarce and very expensive. There were no homes built in the Cove from 1942 to 1945. All industries contributed or converted to help the war efforts. Even the Professional Golf Association cancelled all major golf tournaments.

After the war, the economy changed. The new owners started marketing the cove development as a year-round community and an investment for later development. They did not restrict the sales to Peter Pan members. Glick and Stone did mass marketing campaigns by inviting the starlets from Hollywood to come and enjoy the facilities. They hosted elaborate dinners with complimentary lodging for potential buyers.

The architectural style was beginning to change to accommodate the passing of time and the needs of the buyers. The houses became larger and more ranch style. Pre-WWII simple, linear houses have a less complex form, usually a simple, straight plan with some ornamentation. Post-WWII basic bungalows are simple in plan, larger with less elaborate detailing.

The Desert Club was a huge success. The residences and the visitors alike loved the pool, the dining, dancing, horseback riding, and tennis.

The Desert Club was promoted as:

"Your Club at La Quinta...The Desert Club with its spacious, landscaped grounds is a striking example of California modern architecture. Low, gleaming white and tree encircled, here is a 'ship of the desert': the social hub and playground for La Quinta property owners and guests. Imagine a gorgeous, nature-favored spot where fun and outdoor sports never end. An umbrella dotted swimming pool filled with sparkling, clear, desert water. Low and high diving boards. A separate shallow wading pool for the wee folks. A trim, perfectly kept, tennis court. Badminton, ping-pong, croquet. Horseback riding among the dunes or exhilarating gallops over the hard packed desert sands. Then, for food fit for the gods, come on inside the Clubhouse. Ah, there's architectural plus culinary perfection. The inviting circular lounge; the smart and intimate cocktail bar; the gracious and well-appointed dining room where heavenly food is a La Quinta tradition. Your club, in short, is one of the finest in America.

James Drury, "The Virginian" spent time with his family at the Club in May of 1970. Rita Hayworth was photographed poolside along with Kirk Douglas...Greta Garbo is said to have frequented the Club along with many others."

The Cove was changing. By 1979, the Desert Club was offering tennis club memberships for $240 per year on four night-lighted courts. With year-round families living in the Cove, the residents were busy working and raising families. There was not time to spend at the Desert Club leisurely playing on a daily basis.

The Desert Club was very important to the original La Quinta casitas. It was all a part of Kiener's exclusive planned club development. Families in the 40s, 50s, and 60s loved their Club and all the social life it afforded their community. The Club went through many financial difficulties, two devastating floods, and many owners. At last, the management could not keep it afloat.

In the 1980s, the Club was closed. The buildings and adjoining grounds were deeded over to the City. The grand old Clubhouse was burned to the ground as a practice fire for the Riverside County Fire Department.

The site has become the Fritz Burns' City Park. The massive front doors and coach lamps were saved and given to the La Quinta Historical Society to be displayed in the museum.

1937 lovely old casita. Mexican blue shutters.

1936 casita with a low, pitched, red-tiled roof with original wooden paneling beneath the gables.

1941 "L" shaped casita. The gabled roof is present on both wings. A single carport is created by an extended roof at one end of the wing. The roof has open eaves.

1937 casita completely hidden by massive vegetation. Beautiful backdrop of the Santa Rosa Mountain range.

1938 "I" shape casita. It has two gabled wings coming out of either side of front. There are dark, stained vertical boards with the gables. The porch and roof have been altered from the original design.

1935 "L" shape multi-level red-tiled shed roof.

CHAPTER SEVEN

MOVING FORWARD

Harry Kiener's plan was a success for its time, considering that the period was right after the Stock Market crash of 1929. The country was in a deep depression. In spite of all that, Mr. Kiener gave La Quinta its first residential district, which is now considered the historical district of La Quinta.

There are 48 pre-war homes listed in the La Quinta Cove Thematic Historic District survey. There were 63 homes built in that time period, but only 48 are listed on the historical survey.

The publication called "Remembering The Desert Club" says it best:

"What these men have accomplished since then is truly a saga of American resourcefulness and ingenuity. Two thousand sun-drenched acres plotted in large and small parcels. Lovely Spanish and California ranch homes basking in the winterless warmth. A smart, richly appointed, club. A beautiful swimming pool with all the glamour and color of a star-studded moving picture set. Yes, La Quinta and the Desert Club are seasoned, long-established realities."

In the 1970s, the Cove became a free-for-all for anyone wanting to build. It was among the most affordable places to build in the Coachella Valley. Houses sprung up like weeds all over the Cove area. Without essential community development, planning, or funding, services such as police protection and refuse pick-up made dealing with crime and garbage a big problem. The Desert Club was struggling; life had changed in the Cove.

The Cove was deteriorating until 1982, when La Quinta became a city. The City of La Quinta paved the streets, installed gutters, created a sewer system, and provided mandatory garbage service. Law and order came to the Cove. Pride in ownership became evident; custom well-built homes were built with well planned landscapes.

Seventy-two years later, the pre-war Spanish Colonial Revival casitas are still very desirable. The casitas have stayed romantic and charming. Their curb appeal is inviting and mysterious. The owners are still captivated by their casitas, which exude that same charming, modest, unpretentious, timeless style of the 1930s and 1940s.

1937 casita, once owned by actress Shirley Booth.

Very old Elephant Foot Palm found in a casita backyard.

Behind the adobe-like walls, this casita has many original features.

Restored in 1937. Modern windows mimic the original.

Old Mexican-style fountain

1937 casita courtyard (photo courtesy of Carol Bruno).

Charming, inviting front yard behind adobe-like walls (photo courtesy of Carol Bruno).

1937 magnificent front patio with "Z" door (photo courtesy of Carol Bruno).

1937 center front patio hidden behind adobe-like wall.

CHAPTER EIGHT

COVE LIFE REMEMBERED

Buddy Yessayian, who grew up in the Cove, conveyed an interesting perspective. He remembers that in the 1950s, there were many vacant lots and few homes; today, that has been reversed. Now, there are many homes and very few vacant lots. Considering that there are approximately 6,000 lots in the Cove, that is an interesting observation.

Rosie Funtas, who owned and operated Rosie's Café (located on Calle Estado near Avenida Burmudas), remembers serving many stars and starlets in her Café. Many of them would rent the little houses. She said they were just regular people.

Wendy Lemmon inherited her little Cove house, which she had known for most of her life. She first came there to vacation as a child; later, she moved to La Quinta full time. Her parents discovered the Cove in the early 1950s. Their friends came to visit and quickly bought their own casitas in the Cove.

Wendy remembers that the Desert Club was the center of recreational and social activity. The Desert Club was a place to swim and meet friends and neighbors for dinner. She remembers hearing that there was gambling in the basement or wine cellar. Across the street from the Desert Club were the stables where she, her family, and her friends would rent horses for rides up into the mountains.

She remembers that there were only three paved roads in the Cove: Avenida Bermudas, Eisenhower Drive, and Avenida Obregon. The rest of the roads were gravel with large berms down the center for flood control. There was also a large berm around the outside of the Cove where the wide, deep wash is now, also for flood control.

There were no curbs or gutters until the 1980s, when La Quinta became a city. Each casita originally had a septic tank. A friend once landed his airplane in the middle of Obregon while coming to visit Wendy's sister, and no one seemed to mind. Until the 1970s, there were no stop signs in the Cove.

When Wendy's parents bought their casita, it was fully furnished. The bedroom had two twin beds with head and foot boards, two nightstands, a vanity, and a stool. The living room had a couch and chair with a matching ottoman and a coffee table. There was a dining table with four chairs, pictures, and brown, orange, and beige striped barkcloth curtains on wrought-iron rods with rings. There were wrought-iron sconces with hurricane glass and wrought-iron caps. The furniture was well made out of hardwood with wrought-iron trim. Wendy still uses many of the furniture pieces today.

There have been two family deaths and two family births in their casita. The original fireplace still remains. The garage has been enclosed and a carport was added. The windows are original. It is obvious that this little house has been loved and enjoyed since it was built in 1937.

Wendy said her family believes that the meaning of La Quinta relates to Point Happy/La Quinta being the fifth Cove from Palm Springs. As a kid, she remembers seeing tarantulas, lizards, coyotes, and snakes. They are a family of hikers. They like to hike to the old stairs cut into the mountain where the movie "The Fisherman" was filmed in 1939. Wendy and her family still reside in the Cove.

Victor Teran grew up in the Cove and owns a casita. When he read that La Quinta is the "Gem of the Desert," he said that his casita in the La Quinta Cove was his jewel.

Vi Messick came to the Cove in 1949, when her husband, Charles, was hired to teach school in Indio. They found housing in the Cove. Within two years, her husband was appointed by President Eisenhower to be the La Quinta Postmaster.

At that time, there was no mail delivery in La Quinta. There were 75 rented mailboxes. She helped her husband in the Post Office, which was first located on Calle Tampico, where the Mexican market is today. Then the Post Office was moved to Montezuma in the two-story building that was built in 1935 to house the La Quinta Milling and Lumber Company. She and her family lived upstairs.

The park had a wading pool. In the park, big cookouts were planned with movies for all the neighbors and friends. She said the Desert Club was a nice place. There were special dinners. It was "like a big family;" the whole neighborhood would attend.

All the small homes built in 1935-1941 for weekenders or winter homes were called "the little houses." There were lots of celebrities at the La Quinta Hotel and the Desert Club, and many of the celebrities used the little houses.

Vi remembers that Kathryn Hepburn often stayed at the Hotel. Miss Hepburn enjoyed her daily walks and always wore a large hat. Vi's young son would play in the front yard with his wagon, and whenever Miss Hepburn passed, she would stop and talk to him. They became friends. She has other stories of famous people, but to this day, she respects their privacy and will not reveal their names or their stories.

President Eisenhower stayed in one of the La Quinta Hotel homes. Mail would come for him, and Vi or her husband would hand deliver it to his quarters at the Hotel.

Later, the Messick family moved to the middle of the Cove. They could sit in their front yard and look down the street to see the backside of the La Quinta Hotel. Her husband repaired the Cove street signs after the kids at the bus stop knocked them down.

Vi remembers that Washington Street was first called Marshall Street. Eisenhower Drive was first called Avenida Serra; it was changed in the early 1960s to honor President Eisenhower. Vi still lives in the Cove.

Rupert Yassayian grew up in the Cove. He owns one of the little Cove houses that were built in 1937. It is currently like its original form. The one-car garage, the wood windows, and the front door all remain the same. He remembers Eisenhower Drive with palm trees all the way up the Cove. Some of the palm trees are still there. He also remembers palm trees on Obregon, from Montezuma all the way up the Cove.

The concrete street signs would fall over from time to time. He remembers the Postmaster, Charles Messick, going out and repairing the signs. There were two street signs at every intersection. Rupert remembered the school bus stopping at the Post Office. He would get off the bus and get his family's mail, re-board the school bus, and ride on to his home. When asked about Hollywood and the Cove, he said that he once sold a casita to actress Nancy Cope. Mrs. Yessayian, his mother, still lives in the Cove.

Velma Springer bought a casita in La Quinta Cove after visiting friends in the early 1950s. She has owned three of the casitas over the years. With each new casita, they would purchase the lot next door. There were many lots, and buildings were sparse. The Desert Club was certainly a huge drawing card for them. They loved getting away from Los Angeles. She was a world traveler, and she desired to live in La Quinta because "there is no place in the world like La Quinta. I prefer La Quinta to any place I have ever lived."

They bought their first little Cove house in the 1950s as a vacation home. Over the years, it got more difficult for them to pack up and return to LA, so they decided to make La Quinta their permanent home. She remembers walking her child to the school bus one morning and discovering fresh mountain lion tracks. She never actually saw a mountain lion, but she knew they were around. Velma still resides in the Cove.

Mary Turner lives in a 1938 casita in the Cove. She is a long-time resident. She remembers a valet at the La Quinta Hotel once getting a tip for $900. She also remembers the Kennedy brothers from Massachusetts staying in a home across the street from her. She said that the very wealthy would come and stay all winter. Mary still resides in the Cove.

Jim Cathcart is co-owner of La Quinta Palms Realty, which is housed in an old casita on Eisenhower Drive at Calle Tampico. Jim told of a lady coming in a few years ago just to see the inside of the office. She told him that she and her husband had owned that casita in the 1940s. They arrived for a vacation. As she was unpacking, she opened a drawer to find a rattlesnake hiding. She immediately ran out of the casita, never to return until that day. The casita was quickly put on the market and sold. Bruce and Jim have restored and maintained their historical casita-office, keeping the original front door and windows.

Shirley Wetherell, a Cove resident, works as a realtor. She tells of being called for a listing appointment by a lady named Betty, who had lived in her Cove casita for a very long time. While they were discussing business on the patio, a roadrunner climbed up on Betty's lap and ate out of her hand. It was business as usual for the owner and the roadrunner.

Mark Harner, a La Quinta banker, told about his grandparents buying a weekend home in the Cove in 1939. His grandfather was an ear, nose, throat, and eye doctor with a hobby of painting. Dr. and Mrs. Harner had a houseguest who was also an artist; he painted a picture of their casita and named it "Hacienda de Harner." Sixty-eight years later, Dr. Harner's grandson hangs that painting in his Old Town La Quinta office. It represents very fond family stories and history. The grandparents only owned their casita for three years before the doctor joined the war effort.

Celeste Sheafe, a casita owner, has been told that her casita's three-car garage was once used as the La Quinta Hotel stables. She had a visitor from the famed Irvine Ranch of Orange County and was told of a relative who had lived there for many years. There was a gift left for the present owner, and pictures of the casita were taken before the visitor departed.

I. B. Kornblum, the late Mr. Kornblum in a taped presentation, told of the La Quinta Cove having telephone service. Each home with service was on a 10-party line. He used to listen in on the party line. Jack Benny and his producer would talk every Saturday, discussing what they would do for his show, which aired the next day. Mr. Kornblum would always know what to expect to see on the Jack Benny show. One day, he met the producer and told him about listening on the party line. They had a big laugh over that.

Louise Neeley, the La Quinta Historical Museum manager, had a visitor last fall who said she was Harry Kiener's daughter. She signed the guest book as Mrs. Louie L'Amour. The visitor did not respond to later inquiries regarding her father.

Julie Scott Hirsch, in "Remembering The Desert Club," tells about John Barrymore. "In 1936, the studio he was under contract to sent him to La Quinta to rest and recuperate in preparation for a new movie they wanted him to star in. Due to his contractual obligations, the studio apparently owned Mr. Barrymore body and soul. Mr. Barrymore was installed in a casita behind our house..." Julie's family has fond memories of Mr. Barrymore being a very nice person.

If only the casita walls could talk, there would be many more stories.

ACKNOWLEDGMENTS

This compilation of bits and pieces of the casita story has been a labor of love. There are few original thoughts in this writing. It is simply piecing together the most accurate facts about these charming, fun La Quinta Cove casitas.

There were some conflicting dates and stories, so I did my best to sort out the most accurate truths and details.

Louise Neeley, the La Quinta Museum manager, was the most helpful and accommodating. The best part is that we became friends. Thanks to Wendy Lemmons, the Yessayian brothers, Victor Teran, Vi Messick, Velma Springer, Chythia Holroyd, Carol Bruno, Sherley Wetherrell, Julie Hirsch, Rosie Funtas, the Cathcart brothers, and John Meager.

A special thanks to my special friend, Lyla Dusing, for proofreading my work. Thank you to our friends, who endured my curiosity and love for these old houses, Jeanne, Elaine, Judy, Ann, Carol, Barbara, Chyrs, Liz and Norma.

Thanks to our sons: Trent, who kept asking to read my story; Baylor, who encouraged me in the beginning; and Sloan, who helped me out of computer jams.

A big thanks to my husband, Bill, for endlessly listening.

Thank you all. These little houses deserve their own place in history. I hope this little story honors them properly.

REFERENCES

Gellner, Arrol

    2002 Red Tile Style

    New York: Viking Studio, Penguin Putnam, Inc.

Internet Resource

    Spanish Colonial Revival – Pre-WWII

Kornblum, I.B

    1960/83 Taped presentation/interview

L.Q. Historical Society Museum

    1996 Hacienda Del Gato: Lore and Legend.

L.Q. Historical Society Museum

    1995 La Quinta's Historic Hotel: Desert Paradise of Peace and Serenity

L.Q. Historical Society Museum

    1996 Point Happy Ranch: La Quinta California

L.Q. Historical Society Museum

    1995 Remembering the Desert Club: La Quinta

L.Q. Historical Society Museum

>1990 <u>The History of...La Quinta: The Gem of The Desert</u>

L.Q. Historical Society Museum

>1991 <u>Presenting La Quinta</u>

L.Q. Historical Museum

>1992 <u>La Quinta: The First Decade 1982-1992</u>

L.Q. Historical Museum

>1938 <u>EL Heraldo de La Quinta, reprint #81</u>

Mellon and Associates

>1997 La Quinta Cove Thematic Historic District Survey

Palm Springs – La Quinta Development Co V. Kieberk Corp. (1941) 46 CA2d 234

Pawley, Dr. Ralph, n.d. The La Quinta area

Personal Interviews: 2006

>Louise Neeley, lifelong resident and La Quinta Museum manager

>Velma Springer, casita owner, longtime resident

>Wendy Lemmons, casita owner, longtime resident

>Julie Scott Hirsch, first casita resident, lifetime resident, daughter of the contractor for the development

Victor Teran, long-time resident, casita owner

Vi Messick, Postmaster's wife, long time resident

Ruport Yessayian, lifelong resident, Cove Realtor, casita owner

Buddy Yessayian, long-time resident, Realtor

Rosie Funtas, long-time resident, owner of Rosie's Café (1952-1963)

Mary Turner, long-time resident, casita owner

Bruce Cathcart, realtor, casita owner

Jim Cathcart, realtor, casita owner

Sherley Wetherell, realtor, cove resident

Velma Springer, casita owner, long-time resident

Celeste Sheafe, casita owner, cove resident

Survey sent to all casita owners, 2006.

Old pictures are the courtesy of the La Quinta Historical Society and Museum, Victor Teran, Julie Scott Hirsch, and Wendy Lemmons.

70 YEARS LATER, we still love our charming little houses. Thank you, Mr. Kiener.